A Picture Treasury
of BARBECUING
A TESTED RECIPE INSTITUTE COOK BOOK

BY THE HOME ECONOMICS STAFF OF

TESTED RECIPE

INSTITUTE,

INC.

Demetria M. Taylor	Home Economics Director
Lillian C. Ziegfeld	Executive Home Economist
Mabel Stolte	Home Economist
Frances H. Hoffman	Home Economist
George M. Gilbert	Art Director
Stanley Robinson	Illustrator
Albert Gommi	Photographer
Annette Rhys	Food Specialist

AND WITH THE COOPERATION OF BARBECUE
EXPERTS OF *Big Boy*® MFG. CO.

Table of Contents

How It All Began

Back in the days of cave men and wandering tribes — when cooking first began — men used to roast or broil their food in the open air. There was no other way to do it. Pioneers, cowboys, and hunters also barbecued, not as a hobby or diversion, but just to eat. As time went on, for most of us, cooking over an open fire was no longer a necessity. Modern inventions brought gas and electric ranges into the kitchen. Still, there's something of the rugged outdoorsman in every American — there's a feeling of adventure and good fellowship about a barbecue that helps to explain its tremendous popularity.

In Texas and other parts of the West and South, there grew up the custom of huge parties, sometimes for thousands of people, where first buffalo and later hogs and cattle were roasted whole, served with mountains of bread and barrels of beer. These "ox-roasts" were usually accompanied with fireworks, games, races, and square dancing — a good time for all.

Today, millions who know that there is no substitute for the true tangy charcoal flavor of a barbecued steak are holding equally festive outdoor parties on a much smaller scale. And it's no wonder barbecues are becoming so popular! They are recognized as the graceful, informal way to entertain. Whether on a penthouse garden, a cool patio, a shady lawn or at the beach, it's a chance in the summer for a woman to get out of the hot kitchen into the open air where cooking is a pleasure and the men often take over. More and more, people are realizing that the fun of a barbecue needn't be restricted to the summer months — that late fall and early spring cook-outs are exciting because of the feel of the crisp air and the smell of the charcoal-barbecued meats. Even in the winter, a barbecue in the garage, a breezeway or any other sheltered spot is possible and fun too.

We at Tested Recipe Institute have selected Big Boy Equipment because we know it is exceptionally fine equipment and will give excellent barbecuing results with a minimum of work and expense. We feel you should use high quality, nationally advertised barbecue fuel. Purchase good quality meats, poultry and other foods in order to make the barbecue an occasion which will be long remembered.

How To Select Barbecue Equipment

The barbecue equipment that will give you and your family the most pleasure and excitement should be quality-built and with the essential features that will bring you real enjoyment. Equipment that is portable allows much greater freedom in planning parties. All Big Boy Equipment is portable and can be moved from the garage, to the breezeway and to the yard when the occasion demands.

A barbecue unit designed so you can control the heat is a necessity if you want to be an expert on out-of-door cooking. All Big Boy units are designed with heat-control features, either adjustable fire boxes or adjustable grills.

Important Features to Look For

- High quality heavy duty steel for durable construction of fire box, brazier, legs and hood.

- Comfortable working height of the barbecuing surface.

- Heavy duty legs braced by a one-piece service shelf.

- Large heavy duty wheels with bushings and heavy duty axles to permit ease in moving equipment to the barbecue area.

- Grill made of steel with copper nickel and chrome finish and closely spaced rods.

- Heavy duty spit assembly with a heavy duty motor which rotates 6 RPM clockwise, for proper self-basting. Spit rods should be about 3/8" square. Spit forks should be made of heavy spring steel. Rod and forks should have copper nickel and chrome finish.

- Mechanism for raising or lowering grill or fire box should have positive type action and be sturdy and well constructed. Never buy a makeshift mechanism as it may result in spoiling expensive meats.

- Quality hood of stainless steel or a heavy duty bonderized cold rolled steel. This type hood insures a maximum of reflected heat for best results. It should extend beyond the center of the grilling area and the spit should be mounted, not in front of, but well inside the hood. This type of hood also protects the meats from wind, will keep them barbecuing evenly and will insure maximum retention of juices.

Equipment having the above features, plus a durable hard glossy finish, will add to your pride of ownership and give you years of barbecuing pleasure. Your barbecue center is a family investment, therefore, we recommend buying those FEATURES which will properly serve your family's needs. Price alone is false economy.

Make Barbecuing a Family Pastime

The Fun of Barbecuing at Home

Everybody pitches in and enjoys the "get-ready" as well as the eating. New acquaintances and neighbors are like old friends after you've cooked a meal together.

Husbands become the experts and do the barbecuing. Wives take it easy. All they have to do is make the salad and dessert. The kitchen stays clean. The house remains neat. There is almost no wash-up afterwards.

You can laugh at bumper-to-bumper traffic on steaming highways as you play host in your own backyard. All the comforts of home, plus the carefree, informal fun of the picnics you loved in childhood!

So economical, too! Serve your friends fine barbecues. The cost is only about $1.25 a person instead of about $5.00 for the same meal in a restaurant.

Pull up the benches and have a big crowd. You can entertain 15 or 20 outdoors with less trouble than it takes for six in the dining room, and with less strain on the budget. On weekends outdoor breakfasts are fun too.

Be the Barbecue Leader in your neighborhood. Your friends will call you the best host in town. Then they'll invite you to their backyards after they've learned your tricks of entertaining in the great outdoors.

How to plan a Barbecue

There is only one way in which a barbecue bears any resemblance to other forms of entertaining, and that is the need for planning ahead.

A few quiet moments with pencil and paper will do away with headaches and confusion on the day of the barbecue. Supplies won't run short, food won't be wasted, serving and clean-up will be simplified enormously, and everyone will have a good time.

First comes the menu. Keep it simple and easy to manage. Put most of the emphasis on the barbecued food and limit other courses to chilled juice cocktail, a crisp salad, an easy-to-eat dessert that can be made ahead of time (such as cake, pie, cookies or ice-cream cones) and plenty of coffee or tea, hot or iced depending on the season. You will find many such menu suggestions scattered through the book.

Next comes the market order. Gauge amounts by the length of your guest list. Plan on two helpings of barbecued foods, but buy enough so that, if a couple of trenchermen are present, they can have three! The information on page 17 will help you to decide how much meat to buy.

Now make a list of all the preparation jobs that can be done ahead of time — dessert, salad ingredients, breads, etc. Then list on-the-spot jobs and jot down a name opposite each so everyone can get in the act.

Check all of your barbecuing and serving equipment to be sure that everything is in good condition.

Whenever possible (and it usually is) use paper dishes and cups to make clean-up easy. Choose sturdy, plastic-coated plates that won't disintegrate when hot food is served on them, and get special strong paper cups for hot beverages — never use wax coated cups except for cold beverages. Man-sized, tough paper napkins, and plenty of them, are a must for barbecues. Use stainless steel table cutlery with raffia-wrapped or bright plastic handles to spare your fine silver.

Use the right kind of fuel and you don't need to worry. Proper fuel will minimize flame-ups and smoke. If it rains, set up the equipment in a breezeway or a well-ventilated garage.

Fun for everyone in all kinds of weather . . . bright breezy spring days, lazy summer evenings when daylight lingers long, crisp blue and gold autumn weather, sunlit frosty winter days . . . even when it rains or snows . . . because a barbecue awakens the gypsy in all of us with its light-hearted informality and comradeship.

Equipment Check List

For the Fire

Gravel
Charcoal briquets
Big Boy Fire Starters
    Electro-rod
    Golden Flame Starter
    E-Ze-Lite Starter
Charcoal lighter fluid
Fire rake
Fire tongs
Pail of water (for
    quenching briquets)
Asbestos gloves
Small shovel
Smoke chips
Matches

For Spit Barbecuing

Spit motor or spit crank
Spit rod
Spit forks
Spit basket
Skewers
Heavy twine
Hammer
Pliers
Heavy duty aluminum foil
Big Boy Barbecue
    Thermometer
Heavy duty extension cord
Basting brush

For Handling Food

Long-handled fork
Long-handled spatula
Long-handled steak tongs

Things You May Need

Salt and pepper and other
    seasonings you may want
Pans (for sauces, etc.)
Coffee pot
Carving board or small
    butcher's block
Carving knife and fork
Platters
Salad bowl
Salad servers or tongs
Trays
Paper plates and cups
Paper napkins
Paper toweling
Paper disposal bags
Knives, forks and spoons
Ice bucket
Thermos
Folding chairs and table
Apron
Sponge
Canvas cover to protect
    grill when not in use

My Own List

CHARCOAL BROILING is man's favorite way to prepare steaks and other meat. Good charcoal fires are easy to make and use if you carefully study and follow the information below and on the following pages.

Facts About Charcoal Briquets

High quality charcoal briquets produced by nationally advertised manufacturers are made from maple, birch, beech, oak and elm trees. These briquets are superior because they are made from hardwoods which are dense and have a low resin content. This results in charcoal briquets which have a minimum of tar and therefore smoke less and have little odor.

Six tons of green, fresh-cut wood is required to produce about one ton of charcoal. The hardwood logs are cut up into chips and placed in a dryer where the heat removes the moisture from the wood. The dry chips are then carbonized into charcoal in huge retorts with a heat of 700 to 900 degrees. Direct flames do not come in contact with the wood chips. The charcoal is then cooled, pulverized, mixed with a binder, and compressed to form the briquets. These briquets are very hard and dense. They will burn for a long period of time giving intense, even heat without "pop sparks." High quality charcoal briquets are essential for a successful barbecue and in the long run will prove to be economical.

Facts About Other Charcoals

Ordinary soft wood or wood scrap charcoal can be used. This charcoal is made by charring wood in a kiln. It comes in varying size chunks, and has a tendency to sputter and smoke and may give the food an undesirable flavor because of a high resin content. Often it will give off "pop sparks" and heat from it may be uneven. If you have difficulty in starting the fire, next time try a different brand of fuel.

We Recommend hardwood charcoal briquets for the best results and the most uniform barbecuing.

Charcoal and charcoal briquets must be stored in a dry place so they will not absorb moisture and become difficult to light.

All About—HOW TO BUILD A FIRE
Properly Designed Equipment Gives Best Results

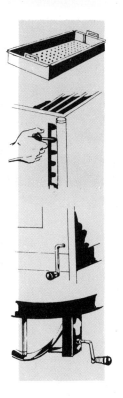

Big Boy Fire Box: These specially designed fire boxes are made of cold rolled steel, welded at all joints. Fire boxes on new models are perforated on the bottom. Others are perforated on the sides. BIG BOY fire boxes are equipped with a screw-type or notch-type elevator assembly (as shown at left) to raise and lower the fire. For, just as you need a thermostatic control on the oven for roasting meats, you need a device for regulating heat when barbecuing.

Fire Bowl of Big Boy Brazier: The fire bowl of every BIG BOY brazier is made of extra-heavy one-piece die-formed steel and has a bonderized baked-on paint finish. Raising or lowering the grill of the brazier, by means of the screw-type mechanism, controls the heat intensity during grilling. But, when using the brazier for spit barbecuing, the heat intensity is controlled by the size of the fire.

Use of Gravel: A gravel base permits fire to "breathe" and gives a more even heat distribution. In all brazier bowls use enough gravel to 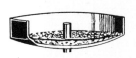 make the bed level out to the edge of the bowl. The fire boxes on the newest model Big Boy barbecue units are perforated on the bottom and sides. These perforations allow the fire to "breathe," thus making the use of gravel unnecessary. If the bottom of the fire box is not perforated, cover it with gravel from 3/4 to 1 inch deep.

Before putting the gravel in the bowl or fire box, line with aluminum foil, if desired. This gives additional fuel economy, reflects the heat and makes cleaning easier. After four to six barbecues, sift gravel and wash in hot water; spread it out to dry. Some gravel "pops" if used when wet, so be sure you dry it before using it again.

Use any gravel (small round stones) or crushed stones 1/4 to 3/8 inch in diameter. These sizes give better barbecuing results.

All About—HOW TO BUILD A FIRE
Three Ways to Start the Fire

Big Boy Electro-rod 720

Method No. 1 BIG BOY ELECTRO-ROD

Arrange a layer of briquets over an area about 8 by 10 inches. Place the heating element of Big Boy Electro-rod in the center. Now put briquets on top of the element to form a pyramid about 5 inches high. Plug Electro-rod into the appliance outlet on spit motor or into an electric outlet. (If extension cord is used, it must be heavy enough to carry 900 W.) After about 7 minutes, gray ash will appear on briquets around the heating element. Remove Electro-rod and disconnect it. Wait about 15 minutes until briquets are well covered with gray ash. Next, arrange them for grill or spit barbecuing as directed on page 12.

Method No. 2 BIG BOY GOLDEN FLAME STARTER

Arrange a pyramid of briquets about 12 inches in diameter and 5 to 6 inches high. Follow instructions on the tube of Big Boy Golden Flame, made by "Golden Touch" Products, Inc., Boston, Mass., from which we quote: "Squeeze small amounts of Golden Flame, (each about the size of 25¢ coin) between the pieces of charcoal or briquettes at a few places. Light each spot with a match." Wait until briquets are covered with gray ash before starting to barbecue. See page 12.

Method No. 3 BIG BOY E-ZE-LITE STARTER

Use E-Ze-Lite Starter, a wax-like substance in a small paper cup, distributed by Big Boy Mfg. Co., Burbank, Calif. We quote from their instructions: "Ignite one lighter cup at point where rim is flared out. Place cup face up where fire is to be built. Make small heap of charcoal or briquets around and over burning cup leaving a little air space. Wax-like substance burns 10 to 15 minutes, thoroughly igniting fuel." Wait until briquets are covered with gray ash before starting to barbecue. See page 12.

All About—HOW TO BUILD A FIRE
How Charcoal Briquets Burn

Because charcoal briquets ignite first in small areas you may think the briquets are not burning. But look closely and you will see tiny gray spots which show where the briquets are burning. To prove to yourself that these gray areas are actually burning, pick up a briquet with a pair of tongs, blow on it and you will see a red glow.

As the briquets burn, a deposit of fine gray ash is left on the surface of the coals. The heat is released through the ash in the form of infra-red rays. In the daytime, the red glow is not normally visible, but when barbecuing with a hood it is sometimes possible to see the glow. At night the red glow is visible.

Fine Gray Ash Acts as an Insulator

Remove this gray ash just before starting to barbecue. Tap the coals lightly with a fire rake or poker. It is also advisable to tap the briquets occasionally during barbecuing to remove the ash. Experiment by putting your hand over briquets that are ash covered. Then tap off the ash and again put your hand over them. Feel how much more heat you have. By this simple device, you often avoid adding more fuel near the end of the barbecuing.

When to Start Your Fire

A good barbecue chef starts his fire far enough in advance to get a good bed of coals before beginning to barbecue. When using a Big Boy Electro-rod, allow about 15 minutes. With other fire starters, allow about 45 minutes. This permits time for the briquets to develop intense heat to cook food properly.

How to Add Charcoal Briquets

Put a supply of briquets in the fire box, at the edge, to warm up. Add warm briquets about 15 minutes before you need them. Do not dump cold briquets on live ones. This reduces the temperature of the fire and retards barbecuing.

To Avoid Flame-Up

On braziers and grills (other than Slant-Grills) move briquets 1/2 inch apart to reduce flame-up when fat drips.

11

Start barbecuing when the charcoal briquets are covered with a fine gray ash. This will take about 15 minutes with the Electro-rod and about 45 minutes with other starters. There will be no visible flame.

Arrange Briquets this Way for the Spit:

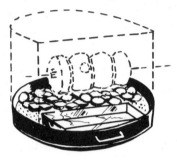
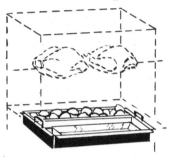

Fig. 1   Fig. 2

Heap briquets in a pile toward the rear of the brazier bowl (see Fig. 1) or fire box (see Fig. 2). If the fire box has a divider, put briquets in back of it. Tap briquets to remove the gray ash. Then, set a drip pan in front of them (see page 15). Attach the spit and start the motor. You can control the amount of heat during barbecuing by adjusting the height of the fire box or by adding or removing briquets in the brazier bowl. After barbecuing starts, it may be necessary to adjust the position of drip pan to catch the juices which drip from the lowest part of the meat.

Arrange Briquets this Way for the Grill:

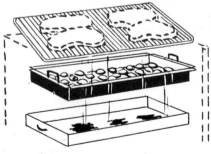

Fig. 3   Fig. 4

Spread the briquets over the gravel in the brazier (see Fig. 3) or in the fire box (see Fig. 4), leaving about 1/2 inch space between the briquets to avoid flame-up. Tap briquets, if necessary, to remove gray ash. If you are using the Slant-Grill, it is not necessary to space briquets to avoid flame-up. Fat runs down grill rods into catch pan below.

All About—HOW TO BUILD A FIRE
Factors Which Influence Barbecuing Time

Kind of Fuel: Charcoal briquets burn with an intense, even heat for a long period of time. Inferior fuels may burn too fast or too slowly. Poor fuels may sputter and smoke, "pop spark" or flame and you will miss the true charcoal flavor. You can easily spoil an expensive cut of meat by experimenting with unproven fuels. With good charcoal briquets giving the same even heat each time, you will learn to depend on them for more exact timing of your barbecued foods.

Amount of Fuel: The degree of heat from charcoal briquets depends on how many briquets are used and how closely they are placed together. Learn how to use a modest quantity.

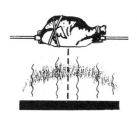

Size and Shape of Meat: Barbecuing time will vary considerably depending on the size and shape of the meat to be barbecued.

Distance of Food from Heat: Place your hand close to burning charcoal briquets and gradually draw it away. You will see that the distance of the food from the heat will make a lot of difference.

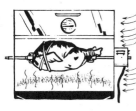

Wind Velocity and Direction: The hood of your Big Boy unit will protect the food from the wind. To prevent the top of the meat from cooling while the underside is barbecuing, turn the back of the hood into the wind.

Because of these Factors, all barbecuing times given are estimates based on average conditions. Keep records of what you do for your own future guidance.

When You Are in a Hurry: Build a fire following one of the methods described on page 10. When the first gray spots appear, use one of the appliances below to create a movement of air. This gives a bed of coals in 5 to 10 minutes. We suggest using this method only in an emergency. Never do this after your meat is on the spit or grill.

Hand operated bellows   Electric fan
Electric hair dryer   Battery operated blower

Smoking For Flavor

In the romantic past, when all the landed gentry prided themselves on well-stocked larders, the smokehouse was an asset no one could be without. Hams, bacon and other meats hung in the aromatic smoke, taking on delectable flavor, until properly cured.

Today, with Big Boy equipment and smoke chips, smoking foods is fun. Not just ham and bacon, but sausages, spareribs, poultry and fish, can be smoked to perfection. And you can control the amount of smoke flavor by the quantity of chips you use as well as by the heat of the fire. Long, slow smoking intensifies the flavor. And, smoking not only adds flavor, but preserves the natural juices so that the meat will keep longer.

Smoke chips are a flavoring agent, not a fuel. Use hickory, walnut, cherry, apple, or any other nut or fruit woods.

Smoking On Any Equipment

This method imparts a slight smoke flavor to any grill or spit barbecued foods.

Soak a handful of smoke chips in water for at least 20 minutes. This increases the amount of smoke penetration and prolongs the life of the chips.

When the fire is ready (see page 12), place a few of the soaked chips directly on the briquets. As soon as chips flame-up remove them with tongs and drop in water. Then, add a few more dampened chips to the fire to continue the smoking process.

Old-Fashioned Covered Smoking

The pork loin roast on page 39 was hickory smoked in the Big Boy Unit DL200. This may also be done in any unit on which a smoker adapter can be used.

Soak a handful of smoke chips at least 20 minutes, as directed above. Meanwhile, following directions on page 12, heap the burning charcoal briquets toward the rear portion of fire box and place a drip pan under

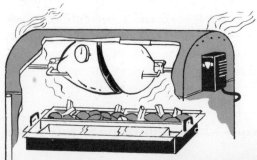

food to be smoked. Then, place the soaked smoke chips on the briquets as above. Put the meat, poultry or fish on the spit rod. Attach the spit; start the motor and lower the cover on the smoker.

Foil Drip Pans for Spit Barbecuing

• Catch fats and juices for making gravies or sauces to serve with the meat.

1. Take an 18″ roll of heavy duty aluminum foil. Tear off two sheets, each about 5″ longer than the meat on the spit. Lay one sheet on top of the other.

2. Fold in half lengthwise. Now you have four thicknesses of foil, 9″ wide and 5″ longer than the meat.

3. Form the sides and ends 1½″ high. Use a cutting board or paste board box to make a neat square fold. Pull out the corners from the sides as shown.

4. Fold the corners back against the sides. This leaves the inside seams tight and smooth, so drippings will not leak out.

5. The finished tray is about 6″ wide, has sides 1½″ high. The 4 corners are square and leakproof. The pan is now ready to place under the meat on the spit.

Place the aluminum foil drip pan parallel to and slightly forward of the spit rod in all spit barbecuing. Make sure the drip pan does not rest on the burning briquets.

For the Big Boy Slant-Grill units, line the drawer-type catch pan with aluminum foil for easier cleaning.

See page 64 for the recipes which require use of a drip pan.

How to Select Meat

Meat for a barbecue should be choice meat, such as you would select for roasting or broiling. Only an expert can judge quality by appearance, so it's better to rely on your local meat dealer.

Beef: Top quality beef is dull red, marbled with streaks of fat throughout the lean, with an outer coating of firm, white fat.

Standing Rib Roast: There are usually 7 ribs in the rib section of beef. Never buy less than a 2-rib roast, which will serve 4. With each additional rib you can serve 2 more people. For best results have short ribs cut off and the flank turned over and tied (see page 34).

Rolled Rib Roast: This is a rib roast, boned, rolled and tied. Ask the meat dealer to roll the beef around a piece of fat, and to roll extra fat around the outside, before tying. Never buy less than a 4-pound rolled roast, which will serve 4 people.

Porterhouse or T-Bone Steak: These are tender and flavorful, but not as easy to carve for a crowd as sirloin. Use steaks from 1½″ to 2″ thick.

Sirloin Steak: Buy a steak from the round end, called the wedge-bone sirloin, for a crowd. Select a steak from 1½″ to 2″ thick.

Club Steak (Delmonico or Shell Steak): These are small steaks with little or no bone. The average 1½″ club steak weighs about 1¼ pounds.

Fillet of Beef (Tenderloin): This is always tender and easy to carve. A whole tenderloin weighs 4 to 6 pounds.

Hamburger: Buy lean ground beef, or boned chuck and have it ground.

Ham: Buy a fine, mild-cured, ready-to-eat ham for a barbecue. It will take 1½ to 2 hours on the spit to barbecue a ready-to-eat ham.

Leg of Lamb: This roast usually weighs 6 to 8 pounds. Spring lamb is best and usually can be purchased all year long.

Chicken: For whole or halved broilers, your best buy is meaty, tender, ready-to-cook birds that can be bought fresh or ice-chilled, or quick-frozen in a package. **Never buy hens for barbecuing.**

Chicken may also be purchased in parts. The breasts, drumsticks, thighs, and possibly wings, are suitable for the barbecue.

Turkey: Again, your best buy is the ready-to-cook bird. Today, turkeys are available in many sizes, from the broiler-fryers (3 to 4 pounds) and small roasters (5 to 8 pounds), to the larger young hen (12 to 16 pounds) or tom turkeys (18 to 30 pounds) ready-to-cook weight.

Duckling: Buy ready-to-cook ducklings, weighing 5 to 6 pounds.

Lobster: The most desirable lobsters weigh from 1 to 2 pounds each. Be sure they are alive when purchased. Split the lobsters yourself or, ask the dealer to split and clean them for you.

How Much Meat To Buy

Outdoor appetites are healthy appetites and the ordinary recommendations as to how much meat to buy, per person, are apt to be on the skimpy side. For a barbecue feast it is better to err on the side of abundance than to let anyone go hungry.

The cut of meat and preparation of it by the meat man influence the amount you buy. When purchasing meat with bone in, such as standing rib roast of beef, leg of lamb or porterhouse steak, you'd better count on from 3/4 to one pound per person. If the meat has no bone or has been boned, (hamburg, top sirloin for shish kebobs and rolled roast of beef) then from 1/3 to 1/2 pound per person is generally sufficient.

Use the following suggestions as a general guide.

Beef: In purchasing porterhouse and sirloin steaks, have them cut about 1½″ thick. If the menu calls for club or rib steaks, allow 1 steak per person and they should be at least 1½″ thick.

Never barbecue less than a 2-rib roast or a 4-pound rolled rib roast. Fillets of beef weigh on an average of 4 to 6 pounds. Half of a 4-pound fillet is the smallest piece you can satisfactorily barbecue.

Pork: Buy two 1-inch rib pork chops per person or 1 to 1½ center-cut chops. Allow about 1 pound of barbecued spareribs per person. You can barbecue a whole pork loin weighing up to 10 pounds or a part of one.

Barbecue at least a half a ham if it has the bone in. You can get a piece with the bone in suitable for barbecuing which weighs as little as 6 pounds; if it's boned use a 4- to 5-pound piece.

Lamb: When serving lamb chops, buy 1 or 2 for each guest depending on whether they are 2″ or 1½″ thick. Never barbecue less than half a leg of lamb. Have steaks cut from the leg, 1″ thick and allow 1 steak per person.

Poultry: The rule for broilers is a half per person. For whole chicken or turkey allow 3/4 of a pound per person. For chicken parts, barbecue a whole breast, 2 to 3 drumsticks or 2 thighs per person. Rock Cornish game hens vary in size. Their weights range from 12 ounces to 3 pounds. So, follow the rule of one small hen per person, or a half or quarter of a larger one. For duckling allow 1/2 per person.

Fish and Seafood: For fish fare, allow 1 whole small fish such as rainbow trout or about 1/2 pound of a large fish for each guest.

You'll want one small lobster or half a large one per guest or 1 pound of rock lobster tails and when shrimp is the dish, have on hand 1/2 pound (uncooked) per guest.

How to Use a Spit

Standing Rib Roast of Beef

Step 1. As shown in Fig. 1, have meat sawed through backbone to free ribs. Insert suet in cut area. Saw through ribs about 2½ inches from ends; remove small bones. Leave meat attached to form a flap; fold over bone ends. Tie roast at 1-inch intervals with heavy twine (Fig. 2).

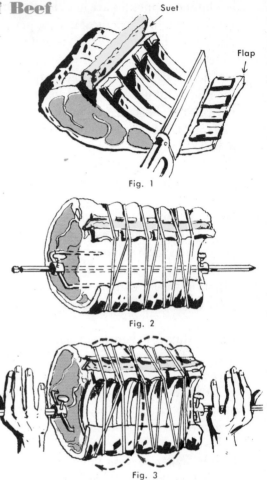

Fig. 1

Fig. 2

Fig. 3

Step 2. Slip a spit fork on rod. Insert point of rod through thickest part of meat (Fig. 2). Put second fork on rod; insert both into meat. Center meat on rod. Tighten fork screws slightly.

Step 3. Test large pieces of meat and poultry for balance by rotating spit rod on palms of hands (Fig. 3). Tighten fork screws with pliers.

Pork Loin

Cut a pork loin into 3 equal pieces, see page 39 or leave whole. Following Step 2 above, arrange meat on rod with a spit fork at both ends of each piece. Test for balance, see Step 3 above.

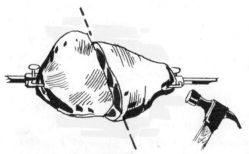

Ham

Have ham cut in half diagonally (Fig. 4). Put a spit fork on rod. Run rod through ham, offsetting butt end for better balance. Put second fork on rod and insert forks in ham; if necessary, use a hammer. Test for balance, as above. Center meat. Tighten screws.

How to Use a Spit

Leg of Lamb

Have 3 inches of bone sawed from small end of leg. Leave meat around bone intact to form a flap. Put a spit fork on rod. Fold flap up and run rod through flap and leg. Put second fork on rod and insert one in each end of leg. Test for balance (see Step 3, page 18). Tighten screws.

Turkey

Step 1. Lay turkey breast side down. Bring neck skin up over neck cavity. Turn under edges of skin; skewer to back skin. Loop twine around skewer and tie. Turn breast side up. Tie or skewer wings to body.

Step 2. Put a spit fork on rod. insert rod in neck skin parallel to backbone; bring it out just above tail. Put a second fork on rod. Insert forks in breast and tail area. Test for balance. Tighten screws. Tie tail to rod with twine. Cross legs; tie to tail.

Single Chicken

To prepare a single chicken for spit barbecuing, follow Steps 1 and 2 for Turkey, above. Be sure chicken is centered on the rod.

Three Chickens on a Spit

Tie or skewer wings to bodies. Put a spit fork on rod. Dovetail chickens on rod. Loop twine around tails and legs; tie to rod. Put second fork on rod; insert forks in end chickens. Tighten screws.

How to Use a Barbecue Thermometer

There are several ways to determine when a roast or large piece of meat is done, but the really accurate way is to use a Big Boy Barbecue Thermometer. The sturdy pointed metal end or tip will never break off and always gives an accurate reading. So insert the Barbecue Thermometer at an angle so the pointed end rests in the center of the thickest part of the meat. Be careful that it doesn't touch the spit or the bone and that the point is not resting in fat, or you will get a false reading.

Then leave the thermometer in place while the meat revolves. Reduce the fire just before the desired temperature is reached. The meat will continue to cook. When the pointer reaches the proper place on the dial, the meat is done. Remove the thermometer and take the meat off the spit.

THE RIGHT WAY

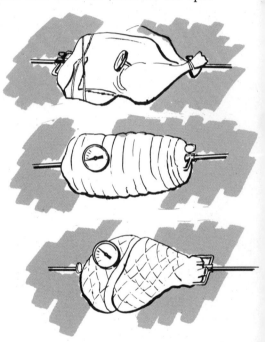

Poultry: Insert tip of thermometer in thick part of thigh close to the body or in heavy part of breast; see diagram right, Turkey page 31 and Chicken page 28.

Rolled Roast: As shown at right insert thermometer so tip is in center of the roast. Take care the tip does not touch the spit.

Ham: Diagram at right and pictures on page 38 show the thermometer inserted in the middle of the heaviest section of the ham.

Other Meats: For placement of thermometer, see Standing Rib Roast of Beef page 34, Leg of Lamb page 42 and Pork Loin page 39.

THE WRONG WAY

Too near the surface— not in center of meat.

Pointed end rests in fat —reading will be high.

Pointed end of thermometer touches spit —reading will be high.

End of the thermometer touches bone — reading will be high.

Barbecue Sauces—Spicy and Savory

Good sauces have great importance in barbecuing certain meats. So, why not become an expert on the making of sauces. We prefer a sauce that enhances the meat flavor but does not overpower it. The recipes on page 22 are among our top favorites, but you may have one that you prefer above all others. If so, by all means continue to use it. If not, try one of ours as a guide, altering it to suit your own taste.

When barbecuing roasts or poultry on the spit, we personally prefer to apply the sauce generously during the last few minutes of the barbecuing period. Besides adding flavor, it keeps the meat moist and appetizing. When applied in this way, you taste the sauce and the meat separately. If you baste constantly while barbecuing, you taste only the condiments in the sauce — the meat flavor will lose its identity. In addition, if the sauce has tomato as an ingredient, it will burn and char long before the meat is cooked.

Try a marinade for such meats as steaks, lamb chops and other small cuts. Cover the meat with marinade, then chill in the refrigerator for several hours or overnight, turning it once or twice. After draining the meat, let come to room temperature before barbecuing.

Some barbecue chefs prefer their meats with a crisp dark brown crust. Kitchen Bouquet heightens the charcoal flavor and increases browning of meats and poultry. Use it just as it comes from the bottle; brush evenly all over the meat with a pastry brush, before barbecuing. Baste occasionally during barbecuing. For additional richness, blend 2 teaspoons of Kitchen Bouquet with 1/4 cup softened fat; use as directed above.

A glaze for barbecued ham, such as our Pineapple Glaze, makes it beautiful as well as flavorful.

Recipes on page 22 are ones we used in barbecuing the meats pictured in this book. Try them, then make your own special variations.

Barbecue Sauces

Marinade

1½ cups salad oil
3/4 cup soy sauce
1/4 cup Worcestershire sauce
2 tablespoons dry mustard
2¼ teaspoons salt

1 tablespoon coarse, freshly ground
  black pepper
1/2 cup wine vinegar
1½ teaspoons dried parsley flakes
2 crushed garlic cloves, if desired
1/3 cup fresh lemon juice

Combine all ingredients and mix well. Make about 3½ cups.

Marinade can be drained from steaks or chops for a second use. Store in a tightly covered jar in freezer indefinitely, or in refrigerator for 1 week.

Easy Basting Sauce

Combine **1/3 cup wine vinegar, 1/3 cup fresh lemon juice** and **1/3 cup salad oil.** Add **1/2 teaspoon soy sauce** and **coarse, freshly ground black pepper** and **salt** to taste. Mix well. Makes 1 cup.

Barbecue Sauce

2 bottles (14 ounces each) ketchup
1 bottle (12 ounces) chili sauce
1/3 cup prepared mustard
1 tablespoon dry mustard
1½ cups firmly packed brown sugar
2 tablespoons coarse, freshly
  ground black pepper
1½ cups wine vinegar

1 cup fresh lemon juice
1/2 cup bottled thick steak sauce
Dash Tabasco, or to taste
1/4 cup Worcestershire sauce
1 tablespoon soy sauce
2 tablespoons salad oil
1 can (12 ounces) beer
Minced or crushed garlic, if desired

Combine all ingredients except the garlic and mix well. Pour into pint jars to store. This sauce may be stored for several weeks in the refrigerator. For longer storage, freeze in freezer. About an hour before using the sauce, add the garlic if desired. Makes about 6 pints.

Pineapple Glaze

1 can (8 ounces) crushed pineapple
1 cup firmly packed brown sugar
1 tablespoon prepared mustard

1 teaspoon dry mustard
Juice of 1 lemon
Dash of salt

Drain syrup from pineapple and reserve. Combine drained pineapple and remaining ingredients and stir to mix well. Add as much of the reserved syrup as necessary to have the mixture of good spreading consistency. Brush over meat during the last few minutes of barbecuing. Makes about 1½ cups.

How do you like your Steak?

Steak is the favorite food of Americans of all ages, both male and female, and has been ever since the first prime steer came off the mid-west ranches. And charcoal broiling is certainly the preferred way to prepare steaks.

Some connoisseurs, self-appointed or elected, shudder at the thought of cooking steak beyond the rare stage. Frankly that's our choice, for we like steak with a "just cooked" flavor and good red color. But each to his own taste we say. So, cook steaks the way you and your guests like them. These pictures tell the story.

RARE

This steak has been over the fire just long enough to sear it and heat it. All the natural juices are sealed in and the color in the center is still a bright red but meat is not raw.

MEDIUM

With longer grilling, the steak loses some of the bright red color but still retains all the natural juices.

WELL DONE

After still longer grilling, the characteristic red color of the beef is gone. The steak is less juicy and thinner. Long barbecuing has cooked out some of the natural juices.

Memos from Big Boy

Grilling Steaks

Always bring steaks to room temperature before grilling. This makes it easier to estimate barbecuing time and gives a more uniformly barbecued steak.

Turn a steak only once, always use tongs or a wide spatula for turning. A fork pierces the meat and lets the juices escape.

Steak should lie flat during barbecuing for best results. If you have had the problem of steak curling, we suggest that before barbecuing, you slash the fat edge at 1½-inch intervals. But, be careful that you do not cut into the meat or you will lose precious juices.

To sear or not to sear steaks, the choice is yours. Tests show that if meats are barbecued to the rare or medium stage they retain their juices whether or not they are seared. However, searing heightens charcoal flavor.

We prefer to season our steaks, except marinated ones, after barbecuing with salt and coarse, freshly ground black pepper. However, some folks like to season the barbecued side of steak immediately after it is turned and complete seasoning the second side when barbecuing is done.

Marinated steaks do not require seasoning after barbecuing.

For garlic-flavored steak, throw a few cloves of garlic on top of the hot briquets while barbecuing the steak.

The Flip Grill and Flipper-Ette

These units are especially suited to barbecuing steaks, chops and hamburgers. No space is needed between pieces of meat for turning. The whole grill, with its contents, flips at once. This eliminates discomfort of heat and smoke which often accompanies the turning of meat with a spatula. The meat-filled grill acts as a cover over the fire, while the shield reflects heat inward, resulting in unusually fast barbecuing and amazing fuel economy. The Flipper-ette is ideal for picnics, camping, use in fireplace or as a patio warmer.

The Slant-Grill

For the utmost enjoyment in barbecuing steaks, hamburgers and many other meats, the Slant-Grill is tops! You can serve rare, medium and well-done meat all barbecued at one time. By just slanting the grill, excess fat runs down grill rods into a catch pan below and not on briquets. This feature practically eliminates flame-up making it possible to build a hotter fire. A hotter fire is particularly desirable for barbecuing steaks and chops.

Sirloin Steaks on the Slant-Grill

Three huge sirloin steaks fit on the grill with room to spare. Steak sand-wiches for a crowd, ready all at the same time — tender slices of juicy charcoal-flavored steak in frankfurter buns, or between slices of fresh bread — man that's eating!

Buy sirloin of beef from 1½ to 2 inches thick. When 2 inches thick, it is much easier to slice for sandwiches. If the steak is frozen, thaw it completely. Fresh or frozen, it should be at room temperature before barbecuing.

Knock the gray ash off briquets. Adjust grill to horizontal position about 3 inches above the briquets. Arrange steaks on the grill and sear 2 or 3 minutes. Then, slant the grill so the rear edge is about 4 inches above the briquets or just until hot fat runs down the rods and into the catch pan below as the steak bar-becues. When the juices come to the surface, the steak is ready to turn. Lower the grill to the horizontal position. Turn the steak using tongs or a spatula. Sear steak 2 or 3 minutes. Then, slant the grill again to complete barbecuing. If desired, baste steak the last few minutes with Easy Basting Sauce (see page 22).

To barbecue steak 2 inches thick to the rare stage, it takes 10 to 15 minutes total searing and barbecuing time for each side. Allow a slightly longer time for medium and well-done steak. To determine whether steak is done as desired, use a small sharp knife and make a slit alongside the bone. When done, sprinkle with salt and coarse, freshly ground black pepper and serve at once, plain or with Barbecue Sauce (see page 22).

To barbecue steak rare, medium and well-done at the same time follow direc-tions above, except, after searing, raise the grill so the rear edge is 7 to 8 inches above the briquets. Continue barbecuing as above. It takes 10 to 15 minutes total time for each side with the grill slanted to this height.

Big Boy Flip Grill ® Pat. Pend.

Charcoal Grilled Club Steaks

Tender triangles of finest flavor, club steaks broil to heights of flavor on the Flip Grill. No need to let flavorful juices escape by trying to turn steak with a fork—no danger of dropping one or two into the fire—just a flip of the grill to turn them all at once.

Allow 1 club steak for each person and have them cut at least 1½ inches thick. Marinate the steak several hours in Marinade (see page 22) in the refrigerator. Then bring to room temperature.

Knock the gray ash off the briquets and space them 1/2 to 3/4 inch apart. Rub the grill with oil or a piece of fat.

Drain excess Marinade from steaks and lay them on the lower part of the Flip Grill. Put top part of grill over steaks; fasten lock securely. Put the grill in position, using the lowest notch at the front and a higher one at the back. Sear 2 or 3 minutes and raise a notch or two, front and back, as shown. Continue to barbecue until juices appear on the top surfaces. Then, flip the grill and lower it for 2 or 3 minutes to sear. Raise grill again and barbecue until done. Allow 6 to 8 minutes total searing and barbecuing time for each side. Remove meat from the grill and serve at once.

When using the Flip Grill, Flipper-ette or Slant-Grill, it is possible to have rare, medium and well-done steaks, ready to come from the grill at the same time. Naturally, those nearest the briquets on the lower part of the grill barbecue faster than those farther away.

When using the Flip Grill be sure that the briquets cover the entire area underneath the meat to be barbecued, leaving a small space between the briquets.

If meat is done before serving time, lower the fire box to the lowest position to keep the meat hot without further cooking. It cooks only when juices bubble on the surface.

Barbecued Beef Tenderloin

Tenderest of all beef cuts, the fillet of beef (tenderloin) rotates slowly over hot, hot, charcoal until it is crisp and brown outside, deep pink and juicy within, ready to be cut into thick slices for serving. Something special, indeed.

A beef tenderloin strip solves all steak problems for the host. Since this cut of steak is thicker at one end than the other, in one operation which is simplicity itself, you can cook steak rare, medium or well done. Let your guests have their choice, and cut slices, thick or thin, to suit individual preferences.

Have the meat at room temperature. Put it on the spit, insert the spit forks and test for balance (see page 18).

Arrange briquets at the rear of the spit and knock off the gray ash. Place the drip pan in front of briquets and under the spit as shown below. Attach the spit and start the motor.

Basting during barbecuing is not necessary. The continuous turning of the meat permits constant self-basting and keeps the meat juicy and flavorful.

Allow about 45 minutes barbecuing time. When done, remove the meat from the spit. Sprinkle with salt and coarse, freshly ground black pepper. Cut in crosswise slices and serve at once, plain or with your favorite barbecue sauce. For extra goodness, serve it in sandwiches made of crisp French Bread brushed with Garlic Butter (see page 57).

Rare   Medium   Well Done   Big Boy Unit DL9

Big Boy Unit DL500

Chickens on the Spit

Use whole ready-to-cook broiler-fryers weighing from 2 to 3½ pounds each. Buy chickens uniform in weight when barbecuing more than one. Rub the body cavities with coarse, freshly ground black pepper and put 1 teaspoon salt or more, as desired, in body cavity of each chicken.

See directions on page 19, to arrange chickens on the spit. Fasten the wings to the bodies with skewers, or tie firmly to the body with twine. Bind legs together; loop twine around tail and fasten to rod. Tighten spit fork screws with pliers. Rub outside of chickens with oil. Insert barbecue thermometer in thickest part of thigh of the center chicken (see page 20).

Make an aluminum foil drip pan according to directions on page 15. For 3 chickens the drip pan should be as long as the fire box. Knock the gray ash from the briquets and heap them slightly at the rear of the fire box, covering an area as long as the chickens on the spit.

Now attach the spit, start the motor and place the drip pan under the chickens. Keep the fire box at the highest position until the chickens are seared, taking care the skin does not blister. Reduce the heat by lowering the fire box 6″ to 7″ from the chickens. Be sure that barbecuing continues. If juice comes to the surface and bubbles, the chickens are barbecuing. Basting during barbecuing is unnecessary. During the last 10 minutes of barbecuing, baste the chickens with drippings from the drip pan or with melted butter or margarine.

Chickens are done when the thermometer registers 190°. Allow 1½ to 2 hours for 3½ pound chickens, 1 to 1¼ hours for smaller chickens. The meat will have pulled away from the bones, especially at the ends of the legs.

Bubbling juices on the surface of the chickens during barbecuing assures you that the heat from the briquets is right.

Constant self-basting of the chickens, which you have only in spit barbecuing, makes chicken succulent, tender and brown.

Chicken Halves in the Spit Basket

Four chicken halves fit perfectly in the spit basket. Use 2 broilers weighing about 3 pounds each. Have the meat man split them and break the joints so the broilers will be as flat as possible. Rub skin sides and spit basket with oil.

Run the spit rod through the spit basket and lay the broilers in it, skin-side up, so the legs are toward the ends as shown below. Put the basket cover in place but do not clamp it down too tightly. Slip the spit forks on to the rod and into the chicken, with one prong in each chicken leg.

Make an aluminum foil drip pan as shown on page 15. Knock the gray ash off the briquets and heap them slightly at the rear of the fire box. Place the aluminum foil drip pan in front of the briquets.

Attach the spit and start the motor. Keep the fire box at the highest position until chickens are seared, taking care not to blister the skin. Then reduce heat by lowering the fire box 6″ to 7″ from the chickens, but be sure that barbecuing continues. Juices on the surface should continue to bubble as the spit revolves. The constant turning of the chicken keeps them self-basted so that basting while barbecuing is unnecessary.

Stop the spit three times, at well-spaced intervals, with the cut sides of the chicken toward the heat and do not start it again for 15 to 30 seconds. These periods of concentrated heat sear the chicken and seal in the juices.

During the last 10 minutes, baste the chicken with Barbecue Sauce or Pineapple Glaze (see page 22). The total barbecuing time will be about 1 to 1¼ hours. When chicken is fork-tender, remove from the spit basket to a hot platter and keep in the warming oven 10 minutes before serving.

Big Boy Unit DL400

Chicken Parts on the Flip Grill

It is true economy and your guests will be happier if you buy chicken parts rather than cut-up whole chickens when you are barbecuing for a crowd. No one wants the backs or the other bony parts. So, buy drumsticks, thighs, breasts and wings, for a choice of light or dark meat.

Brush the Flip Grill and chicken parts with cooking oil. Arrange chicken parts on grill, **either all skin-side up, or all skin-side down.** For a really big crowd or a small crowd with big appetites, put the pieces close together as no space is needed for turning them. Then, put the top part of the grill over the chicken and fasten lock securely.

Spread briquets over the gravel, allowing 1/2 to 3/4 inch between briquets. Knock off the gray ash. Start the barbecuing with the cut side of the chicken down. Put Flip Grill in place with grill in lowest notch on one side, and several notches higher on the other side. Sear for 3 or 4 minutes. Turn and baste with Easy Basting Sauce (see page 22) or melted butter or margarine. After 3 or 4 minutes, turn and baste on other side. Then raise the grill several notches on both sides. Continue to turn every 3 or 4 minutes and baste after each turn. Frequent basting is necessary on the Flip Grill or the chicken will be dry.

The steady, even heat of charcoal barbecues chicken thoroughly and evenly. Total barbecuing time will be 25 to 30 minutes. (See page 13.) The chicken is done when the meat pulls away from the bone.

Of course, you can use the spit basket for chicken parts too. Follow the same basic directions as given for Chicken Halves in the Spit Basket (see p. 29).

Some barbecue chefs prefer to marinate the chicken several hours before barbecuing. For a marinade, try the recipe on page 22.

Big Boy Flip Grill ®
Pat. Pend.

Barbecued Turkey

What is more handsome than a big tom turkey, weighing up to 30 pounds, turning a crackling golden brown as it revolves on the spit over hot charcoal? Do you prefer light or dark meat? Step right up as the juicy slices fall away from the knife — there's aplenty for all!

Select a ready-to-cook, plump, fresh or quick-frozen turkey. If the turkey is frozen, thaw it completely. Wash inside and outside of turkey well. Remove any pin feathers, oil sac and remaining bits of lung and liver.

For added flavor, rinse the inside with wine vinegar. For a 15 to 20 pound bird, put about 2 tablespoons salt in the body cavity and about 2 tablespoons more salt in the neck cavity. Or, allow a total of about 1 tablespoon salt for each 4 pounds of turkey. If desired, mix the salt with coarse, freshly ground black pepper and cooking oil to make a paste; put into cavities.

Secure neck skin; tie or skewer wings and put turkey on spit rod as directed on page 19. Test for balance (see Step 3, page 18). Insert the barbecue thermometer in thigh close to body or, in heavy part of the breast (see page 20).

Arrange briquets at the back of fire box; knock off gray ash. Place a drip pan in front of briquets. Attach spit and, with the fire box at the highest position, start the motor. Sear the turkey, taking care the skin does not blister. Then, lower fire box so that it is 6 to 7 inches from turkey. Continue barbecuing until done. Juices should come to the surface and bubble.

Allow a total of 12 to 15 minutes per pound barbecuing time, but watch the thermometer. During the last 10 minutes of barbecuing, baste turkey with drippings from drip pan or use melted butter or margarine. Barbecue until thermometer registers 190°. When turkey is done, remove the thermometer and slip turkey off the spit. Before carving, let stand 10 minutes to firm up.

Barbecued Squabs

Twelve delectable, succulent, tender little birds, sizzling and crackling as they rotate above hot charcoal briquets until they are done to a turn. One per person — a Gourmet feast for a special occasion.

Allow one squab per person. Place a piece of salt pork over breastbone and secure it while tying wings to body with heavy twine as shown at bottom of page 19. Before you start, be sure you have an ample supply of spit forks.

When using a unit with several short spit rods, dovetail 3 squabs on each spit. (See Three Chickens on a Spit on page 19.) On units with one long spit rod, you can put 4 or 5 squabs on the rod. One or 2 additional squabs may be barbecued on each rod if placed vertically on it. Center squabs on rod. Insert a spit fork in every other squab to hold firmly; tighten fork screws.

Arrange briquets for spit barbecuing (see page 12). Knock off gray ash from briquets. Use foil drip pan, if necessary. Attach spits and start the motor. Keep fire box at the highest position until squabs are seared, taking care not to blister skins. Then, lower the fire box 6 to 7 inches from squabs.

Allow about 45 minutes barbecuing time. During the last 5 minutes of barbecuing, baste with Easy Basting Sauce (see page 22) or melted butter or margarine to which a little oregano or rosemary has been added.

Barbecued Rock Cornish Game Hens are a gourmet's delight. Have the hens at room temperature before barbecuing. Tie wings securely with twine as directed for Three Chickens on a Spit (see page 19). Put hens on the spit and fasten with spit forks. Barbecue as directed for squabs, until done. Time depends on size. Allow about 45 minutes for small size hens and 1½ to 1¾ hours for hens weighing about 3 pounds.

Barbecued Rabbit

If your acquaintance with rabbit is limited to Hasenpfeffer, broaden it immediately by grilling serving-size pieces of rabbit meat over the intense heat of charcoal. Tender as the finest chicken, but with a difference in flavor that is indescribable, charcoal-broiled rabbit will give you top billing as a barbecue chef par excellence!

Use small rabbits weighing from 2 to 3 pounds; cut into serving-size pieces. If the rabbit is frozen, thaw it completely and bring it to room temperature before barbecuing. Brush the rabbit parts with cooking oil. Or, if desired, wrap a slice of bacon around each rabbit part.

When charcoal briquets are covered with gray ash and very hot, knock off the gray ash. Then, space briquets 1/2 to 3/4 inch apart over the gravel to avoid flame-up. Brush the grill with cooking oil. Arrange the rabbit on the grill. Lower the grill so that it is about 3 inches above briquets. Barbecue the rabbit parts about 15 to 20 minutes on one side. Then, baste with melted butter or margarine and turn. Continue barbecuing 15 to 20 minutes more or until fork-tender. Remove from grill. Season with salt and coarse, freshly ground black pepper. Serve immediately.

Rabbit parts can also be barbecued in the spit basket, on the Slant-Grill, the Flip Grill or the Flipper-ette. When you are using the spit basket allow a little longer barbecuing time than is required for barbecuing on the grill. If you are barbecuing rabbit parts on the Slant-Grill, Flip Grill or Flipper-ette, allow about the same amount of time as for grilling them on the brazier unit.

Big Boy Unit DL6

Barbecued Standing Rib Roast of Beef

Our heritage from across the seas, the Roast Beef of Old England still wears the Royal Crown. Everybody's favorite, men, women and children — you cannot go wrong when you decide to barbecue a standing rib roast.

If you insist on well-done beef, we won't argue the point, but serve ours in a generous slice with the fat golden brown, and the lean a fine rosy red!

When buying a rib roast of beef for barbecuing, allow from 3/4 to 1 pound of meat per serving but never barbecue less than a 2-rib roast. Have the meat man prepare the roast as shown on page 18.

Bring the meat to room temperature and put it on the spit rod. Insert the spit forks; tighten the screws and test for balance. Insert the barbecue thermometer in the center of roast taking care it does not touch the spit or bone, or rest in fat. See page 20.

Arrange the ash-coated briquets at the rear of the fire box and knock off the ash. Place the drip pan in front (see page 15). Attach the spit and start the motor. Keep the fire box at the highest position, until roast is seared. Lower the fire box 6″ to 8″ from the roast, but be sure that barbecuing continues. Juices should come to the surface and bubble constantly. If a garlic flavor is desired, throw several cloves on the hot briquets.

Barbecue until done. Thermometer should read 140°F. for rare, 160°F. for medium and 170°F. for well done. Size of the roast and amount of heat as explained on page 13 determine actual barbecuing time. Generally speaking it takes from 12 to 15 minutes per pound.

When roast is done, lift out thermometer, remove meat from the spit and allow it to firm up before carving.

The accurate way to tell when a roast is done, is to use a Big Boy Barbecue Thermometer.

Barbecued Rolled Roast of Beef

If you are having a crowd for a barbecue and want to make it easy for the carver, or if you plan to serve hot roast beef sandwiches, then choose a boned and rolled rib roast.

Allow about 1/2 to 3/4 pound of meat per person when serving a rolled rib roast, but never barbecue a roast which weighs less than 4 pounds. Have the meat man roll the meat around a strip of fat and put a covering of fat about 1/4" thick around the roast before he ties it with heavy twine. Bring the meat to room temperature before barbecuing starts.

Put the roast on the spit as shown below. Insert the spit forks and tighten the screws with pliers. Then test for balance (see page 18). Insert the barbecue thermometer, as shown.

When the briquets are very hot and coated with gray ash, arrange them at the rear and knock off the ash. Put the drip pan in front. Attach the spit and start the motor. If you want the roast garlic-flavored, cut 1 or 2 garlic cloves in half and throw them on the hot briquets.

If the fire becomes too hot during barbecuing, reduce it by removing some of the briquets.

Juices should constantly come to the surface and bubble. This self-basting makes basting during barbecuing unnecessary. It also keeps the twine from burning. Barbecue the roast until done, using the thermometer as a guide: 140° for rare, 160° for medium, 170° for well done. Allow about 12 to 15 minutes per pound. When meat is done, remove the thermometer. Take meat off the spit and cut in crosswise slices.

Big Boy Unit DL9

Four Economy Beef Quickies

Savory Short Ribs

Short ribs are on the bony side and have considerable fat, so allow at least 1 pound per person. Have the meat man cut them in serving-size pieces. Pour Marinade (recipe on page 22) over them and let stand in the refrigerator over night. Then drain well and reserve the Marinade.

Knock the gray ash from the briquets and space them over the gravel about 1/2″ to 3/4″ apart. Rub the grill with cooking oil or a piece of fat. Place the ribs on the grill about 4″ above the briquets. Grill slowly 25 to 35 minutes, turning frequently.

During the last 10 minutes, baste several times with Marinade. When done, season with salt and coarse, freshly ground black pepper. If desired, serve with Barbecue Sauce (see page 22).

Grilled London Broil

Flank steak is the cut of meat to use for Grilled London Broil. A flank steak weighs from 1½ to 2½ pounds. When buying, allow about 1/2 pound per person. With a very sharp knife, score the steak lightly, crisscross fashion, on both sides.

Knock the gray ash from the briquets and space them 1/2″ to 3/4″ apart on the gravel. Rub the grill with cooking oil and lay the steak on top. Grill about 2″ above briquets, 5 minutes on each side, turning once. Remove from grill. Cut diagonally, across the grain, in very thin slices; season with melted butter or margarine, salt and coarse, freshly ground black pepper. Serve topped with Grilled Mushrooms (see page 55).

Beef Roly Polies

Allow 2 cube steaks for each person. Flatten the steaks and spread them with prepared mustard. Sprinkle with a little drained sweet pickle relish, or, lay on each a candied dill pickle strip. Roll up, fasten with small metal skewers and brush with melted butter or margarine.

Knock the gray ash from the briquets and space them 1/2″ to 3/4″ apart over the gravel. Rub the grill with cooking oil and lay the beef rolls on the grill about 2″ above the briquets. Grill about 10 minutes, turning once. When done, sprinkle with salt and coarse, freshly ground black pepper.

Grilled Cube Steak Sandwiches

When serving cube steaks allow 2 for each person. Heat 1 cup Marinade (recipe on page 22) to a boil. Pour over 8 cubed steaks and let stand about 20 minutes, then drain them well.

Knock the gray ash from the briquets and space them 1/2″ to 3/4″ apart over the gravel. Rub the grill with cooking oil. Lay the steaks on the grill about 2″ above the briquets. Grill about 2 minutes on each side, turning once. Sprinkle with salt and coarse, freshly ground black pepper. Serve in hot toasted, buttered hamburger buns, topped with a little Marinade.

Big Boy Flip Grill ® Pat. Pend.

Grilled Pork Chops

Everyone knows that pork, even pork chops, must be cooked to the well-done stage, but not charred or dried out by rapid cooking.

The adjustable grill makes it possible to broil the chops slowly far above the briquets until done, and then to lower the grill for even, deep gold browning and juicy, tender meat.

Have chops cut about 1 inch thick. Be sure to bring them to room temperature before barbecuing.

Rub the Flip Grill with cooking oil. Arrange chops on lower part of grill; put the top part of it over chops and fasten lock securely.

Space briquets about 1/2 inch apart and knock off any gray ash. Put the grill in place with front lower than the rear, as shown above. Sear chops 3 to 4 minutes on one side. Then, raise the grill several notches, front and back, and barbecue 15 to 17 minutes longer. Flip the grill and lower it for 3 to 4 minutes to sear chops on second side. Raise grill again and continue to barbecue until done, about 15 to 17 minutes. If desired, during the last few minutes of barbecuing time, baste with Pineapple Glaze (see recipe on page 22).

When chops are done the meat should be whitish in color. If necessary, make a cut close to the bone of one chop to determine whether they are done.

If desired, chops may be marinated for several hours or overnight before barbecuing. See page 22 for recipe for Marinade.

Pork chops are also delicious barbecued on the Slant-Grill. Sear the chops with the grill in the horizontal position. Then, slant the grill just enough to allow the fat to run down the grill rods into the catch pan below. Allow 15 to 20 minutes total barbecuing time on each side, turning once.

Barbecued Pineapple Glazed Ham

You've never really tasted ham until you've tasted one that has turned slowly on a spit over the intense heat of charcoal. Tender, pink slices, edged with crisp, golden brown, pineapple glazed fat.

Use either a ready-to-eat or uncooked whole ham. Have ham cut in half, diagonally, for better balancing on the spit (see page 18). This also provides greater surface for penetration of the charcoal or smoke flavors. To smoke ham, put a few smoke chips on the briquets during barbecuing (see page 14).

Remove any rind that is left on the ham. Then, score the fat in a diamond pattern. Put ham on the spit as shown on page 18. Insert spit forks at both ends. Test for balance. Center the meat and tighten the screws with pliers. Insert Big Boy Barbecue Thermometer in the center of the thickest section of one half, as shown above. Be sure it does not touch the spit or bone or rest in fat.

Arrange briquets at rear and knock off the gray ash. Attach the spit and start the motor. Place drip pan under ham. Allow about 10 minutes per pound for a ready-to-eat ham or 25 minutes per pound for an uncooked ham. Baste with Pineapple Glaze (see page 22), during last 15 minutes of barbecuing. When done, meat pulls away from bone. Thermometer should register 140° for a ready-to-eat ham and 170° for an uncooked ham.

Barbecued Boned Roll Ham is a real treat. Remove the casing; tie with heavy twine at 2-inch intervals. Put it on the spit and barbecue as above.

Ham Steaks are delicious when grilled on a brazier. Grill ham steaks 1 inch thick until brown about 8 to 10 minutes on each side, about 3 to 5 inches from the briquets. Baste, if desired, the last few minutes with Pineapple Glaze.

Use an aluminum foil drip pan to catch fats and juices for making gravies or sauces.

Do not let the tip of the thermometer touch the spit or bone and do not let it rest in fat.

Hickory Smoked Pork Loin

Once you use a Smoker, your enthusiasm will know no bounds. Everything from domestic poultry to wild fowl, from various cuts of pork to game meats, even fish, fresh from sea or stream, takes on an exotic flavor. Try barbecuing a pork loin. Permeated with the incomparable flavor of hickory plus charcoal, it will make a barbecue everyone will remember.

When buying a pork loin for barbecuing, allow from 3/4 to 1 pound per serving, but never barbecue less than a 3½-pound loin. Have meat man split backbone between each rib. Bring meat to room temperature. Put pork on a spit rod as directed on page 18. Insert a Big Boy Barbecue Thermometer in cut end of loin as shown in picture below.

To prepare hickory smoke chips see page 14. Or, you may use walnut, apple, or any other fruit wood chips for a delightfully different flavor.

Arrange the briquets at the rear of the fire box and knock off the gray ash. Put a drip pan in front of the briquets. Then, lay the smoke chips on top of briquets as directed on page 14. Attach the spit and, with the fire box 5 to 6 inches below the pork loin, start the motor. Then, lower the smoker cover. The smoking time is approximately the same as required for barbecuing, 30 to 35 minutes per pound. But, for the most accurate guide, rely on the thermometer. It should register 190°. When done, the meat will be whitish in color.

If a very heavy smoke flavor is desired, have meat cut in several pieces, use more hickory chips or, allow a slightly longer barbecuing time for smoking. For a longer smoking period, it may be necessary to reduce the heat.

Big Boy Unit DL200   Pat. Pend.

How to put Spareribs on the Spit

1. Slip one spit fork on the spit rod and turn the screw just enough to keep the fork in place. Beginning with the narrow end of the ribs, run the spit rod through the middle as shown, so that ribs are laced accordion-fashion. Then, push ribs on to the spit fork.

2. Next, start with the wide end of the second rack of ribs and lace it on the spit rod the same as the first rack. Repeat until all ribs are on the spit, starting first with the narrow end of a rack and following with the wide end. Alternating the racks in this way maintains balance.

3. Bring all ribs to the center of the rod and push together as shown. Slip the second spit fork on the rod; tighten screws on both forks with pliers. Run several metal skewers through the ribs, parallel to the spit rod, to hold them securely. Rod is now ready to attach to the motor.

Barbecued Spareribs are done when the meat pulls away from the bones.

This is an accurate guide for perfectly barbecued spareribs, whether they have been done on the spit, in the spit basket or on the grill. See picture at right.

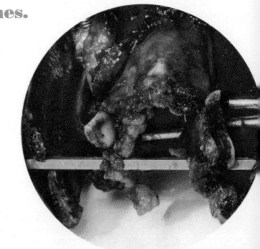

Serve plenty of Barbecue Sauce with the spareribs for dunking. See page 22 for recipe. The combination is even better if the sauce has been warmed.

Barbecued Spareribs

For sheer flavor you cannot beat barbecued spareribs. As they rotate above hot charcoal, sizzling in their own rich fat and browning to a turn, their tantalizing fragrance makes waiting almost unbearable! Finished off with the lusty tang of barbecue sauce, they are truly "out of this world."

Spareribs, like all cuts of pork, must be barbecued to the well-done stage. Because fire conditions and heat from the fire vary (see page 13), be sure to allow plenty of time. You will need from 45 minutes to 1 hour for barbecuing.

For best results, barbecue ribs in a spit basket, or laced on the spit itself. In a spit basket or on a spit, the constant turning bastes the ribs in their own natural juices. For instructions for lacing ribs on the spit, see illustrations on page 40. When barbecuing ribs in the spit basket, slice them apart before arranging them in the basket.

Arrange the briquets at the rear of the fire box or grill (see page 12) and knock off the gray ash. Attach the spit. Place an aluminum foil drip pan in front of the briquets. Start the motor. Barbecue until done (see page 40). If ribs are on the spit, baste them constantly during the last 5 minutes of barbecuing time with Barbecue Sauce (recipe on page 22). When done, slice them apart at once, place individual servings on pieces of aluminum foil and brush generously with Barbecue Sauce. Then wrap and place them in the warming oven or near the briquets to keep warm until serving time.

When barbecuing on the grill, space briquets 1/2 to 3/4 inch apart over the gravel to avoid flame-up. Put the spareribs on the grill. During barbecuing, turn them every 2 or 3 minutes and baste at each turn with a basting sauce. If this is forgotten, the ribs dry out, burn and lose their rich flavor. When done, cut apart, spread with Barbecue Sauce and wrap in foil, as above.

41

Barbecued Leg of Lamb

People who say they don't care for lamb will change their minds promptly at the first taste of a properly barbecued leg of lamb. Faintly aromatic of garlic, delicately flavored with the barbecue sauce, so tender no knife is needed—lamb cooked this way is fit for a king. We like the Scandinavian way with lamb — a wee bit rare so that the slices are more pink than gray.

Select a 6- to 7-pound leg of lamb and have meat man prepare it for spit barbecuing as shown on page 19. Turn the flap of meat up and put it on the spit as directed. Insert the forks. Test for balance and tighten the fork screws with pliers.

Rub the entire surface of meat with cooking oil. Then rub with salt and coarse, freshly ground black pepper. Insert the Big Boy Barbecue Thermometer in the thickest part of the meat as shown above, taking care the tip does not touch the bone, or spit, or rest in fat.

When the briquets are covered with gray ash, knock off the ash. Move briquets to the back of the fire box, heaping them slightly. If a garlic flavor in the meat is desired, throw a few cloves of garlic on the briquets. Attach the spit and start the motor. Set an aluminum foil drip pan in front of the briquets (see page 15) and adjust the fire box to about 6 or 7 inches from the meat. Allowing about 30 minutes per pound, barbecue until done. But watch the thermometer and do not remove the lamb until the thermometer registers 180°. During the last 10 minutes of barbecuing, baste with your choice of barbecue sauces. Remove lamb from spit; let stand 10 minutes before carving to firm up.

The accurate way to tell when a roast is done, is to use a Big Boy Barbecue Thermometer.

This book is an ideal gift for Christmas, anniversaries and special occasions.

Charcoal Grilled Lamb Chops

Twenty — count 'em — twenty plump, juicy lamb chops, turning richly brown, edged with crisp, golden fat — almost ready to serve. Basted with Barbecue Sauce, they are a dish fit for a king.

Center-cut loin and rib lamb chops are most suitable for barbecuing. Have them cut from 1 to 2 inches thick and allow about 2 chops per person. You can, also, grill lamb steaks. Have them cut 1 inch thick and allow 1 per person.

When briquets are covered with gray ash, knock off the ash and space briquets 1/2 to 3/4 inch apart to avoid flame-up. Brush the grill with cooking oil. Arrange chops on the grill. Lower the grill so it is about 2 inches above the briquets; sear chops 1 to 2 minutes. Then, raise the grill so chops are about 3 inches above briquets. Barbecue until ready to turn. Lower the grill to 2 inches above briquets; turn chops and sear 1 to 2 minutes. Raise grill again to 3 inches above briquets and continue barbecuing until chops are done.

For chops about 1½ inches thick, allow about 12 minutes on each side for searing and barbecuing. For chops about 1 inch thick, allow about 8 minutes on each side for searing and barbecuing. When chops are done, season with salt and coarse, freshly ground black pepper.

Of course you can barbecue lamb chops on other units too! For barbecuing chops on the Slant-Grill, Flip Grill and Flipper-ette, allow about the same barbecuing time as you would for the brazier unit. If you are barbecuing lamb chops in the spit basket, allow a slightly longer time.

Big Boy Unit DL6

With the Flip Grill you can easily turn all your meat at one time and have it uniformly barbecued.

Liver, Bacon and Onions

Barbecue liver and bacon? It's really unusual, but why not? The delicate flavor of liver is enhanced by charcoal grilling in a way that lends zest to appetite and eating enjoyment.

Once you have tried it, you will do it again and again. And with the Flip Grill, there is no danger of bacon or onion slices falling on to the briquets.

Use calf or very young beef liver and have it cut 1/2" thick. Liver should be at room temperature when barbecuing begins. Wash the liver and dry on paper towels. Have bacon thickly sliced. Select large Spanish or Bermuda onions. Peel and slice them about 1/2 inch thick. Brush slices with melted butter or margarine. Use firm tomatoes and quarter but do not peel them.

When briquets are coated with gray ash and very hot, knock off the ash and space them 1/2" to 3/4" apart over the gravel to avoid flame-up (see page 10). Rub the Flip Grill with cooking oil and lay liver and onion slices on the lower part. Put top part over the liver and onions and fasten securely. Put the grill in place with one side several notches lower than the other side and the screw attachment face-side down. After about 5 minutes flip the grill. Remove the top and put tomatoes and bacon on the grill. Barbecue about 5 minutes longer. During the last few minutes put onions and bacon on top of liver to blend flavors. Do not overcook the liver.

Big Boy Flip Grill ®
Pat. Pend.

Knackwurst or Bratwurst

Allow about 2 bratwurst or knackwurst per person. Prick each sausage in several places. Arrange on lower part of grill. Put top part of grill in place; fasten lock securely.

Knock ash off the hot briquets and space 1/2 inch apart, keeping them away from front of bowl to prevent flame-up.

Put grill in place with front lower than rear, as shown, so fat will run down grill and drip on gravel instead of on briquets. Barbecue knackwurst a total of 10 to 15 minutes and bratwurst a total of 15 to 20 minutes, turning once. During the last few minutes, baste with barbecue sauce, if desired.

Barbecued Knackwurst

Big Boy Flipper-ette®
Pat. Pend.

Flipper-ette, little brother to the Big Boy Flip Grill, is small and portable, with an unbelievably large cooking area. Spicily hot sausages like knackwurst and bratwurst, given the added flavor of charcoal make wonderful barbecue fare.

There is no need to limit the use of the Flipper-ette to such meats as knackwurst and bratwurst. Any of the foods barbecued on the Flip Grill and brazier-type units are suitable for barbecuing on the Flipper-ette. Just set it on the picnic table. What greater convenience could you ask for!

The Flipper-ette is ideal to use for small parties or as an auxiliary barbecue unit for big parties. Or, just leave it in the trunk of the family car for those "spur-of-the-moment" picnics at the beach or in the woods. Despite its small size, it will hold 6 to 8 hamburgs, 4 to 6 chops, 3 club steaks or 12 to 15 frankfurters at one time.

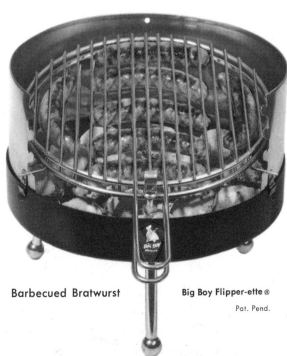

Barbecued Bratwurst

Big Boy Flipper-ette®
Pat. Pend.

Barbecued Shrimp

2 pounds large green
  (raw) shrimp
1/2 cup butter or margarine
1 large garlic clove, minced
1/2 teaspoon salt
1/4 teaspoon coarse, freshly
    ground black pepper
1/2 cup minced parsley

Peel and devein shrimp. Cream butter; add remaining ingredients and stir to mix well. Tear off six 9" strips of heavy duty aluminum foil. Fold each in half to make a 9" square. Divide shrimp equally on pieces of foil. Top each with 1/6 of butter mixture. Bring foil up around shrimp and twist tightly to seal. Knock the gray ash off the briquets. Place shrimp on briquets; barbecue 5 minutes. Makes 6 servings.

Barbecued Lobster

Allow 1 small lobster (1 to 1½ pounds) per person. They must be split lengthwise and cleaned, with the large claws cracked. Have the fish dealer do this for you or, do it yourself for really fresh lobster.

To clean them yourself, lay the lobster on its back shell on a cutting board. At the place where the tail and body come together, insert the tip of a sharp-pointed knife all the way through to the back shell. With a heavy mallet or hammer, crack the large part of each claw. Then, with a knife, make a cut through the center of the thin undershell from head to tail down through the body, just to the back shell, which should be left intact.

Spread lobster open as far as possible. Lift out and discard the dark vein down the center and the small sac, about 2 inches long, just below the head.

When briquets are covered with gray ash and very hot, space them 1/2" to 3/4" apart and knock off the gray ash. Place lobster on the grill, shell-side down 3 or 4 inches above briquets. Barbecue 15 minutes. Brush lobster generously with melted butter or margarine. Sprinkle with salt and coarse, freshly ground black pepper. Turn and barbecue 3 to 5 minutes longer. When lobster is done, shell is bright red. Serve piping hot with melted butter or margarine and lemon wedges.

Big Boy Unit DL6

Big Boy Unit DL6

Charcoal Grilled Rock Lobster Tails

African rock lobster tails are wonderful barbecue fare—they are so easy to cook, to serve and to eat. Peel off the shell and savor the exquisite flavor that is like, yet unlike, our native lobster. One or two of these, with potato salad and hot crispy, French bread, garlic-scented, make a perfect meal.

Select rock lobster tails weighing about 1/2 pound each, buying 2 for each person. Slit lengthwise, if desired. Bend backwards, toward shell side, to crack and prevent curling during barbecuing.

When briquets are covered with gray ash and very hot, space about 1/2" to 3/4" apart over the gravel. Place lobster tails on grill, shell-side down, 3 or 4 inches above briquets. Cook about 15 minutes. Brush generously with melted butter or margarine. Turn and cook 3 minutes longer. Shell is bright red when lobster is done. Season with coarse, freshly ground black pepper and salt to taste. Serve with melted butter or margarine and lemon wedges.

Lobster Tail Canapés

Allow one lobster tail for each guest. Barbecue according to instructions above. When done, remove meat from tail in one piece, leaving the shell intact. Cut the meat from each tail into about 6 cubes and put a cocktail pick in each. Pile cubes into the shells. Serve one to each guest with plenty of Barbecue Sauce (page 22) or your favorite cocktail sauce.

47

Barbecued Small Whole Fish

Rainbow trout is an epicure's dream when cooked in a revolving spit basket over charcoal. There is nothing so fleeting as the delectable flavor of fresh fish. The sooner this flavor can be captured the better.

For campers-out, for one-day fishing trips, for summer colonists at the seashore or near a fresh water stream where small fish abound, Big Boy Portable Barbecue Equipment brings fish from water to table at the height of superb flavor. If you have never tasted brook trout, snappers, small mackerel, bluefish or flounder that have been barbecued over charcoal, then you have never tasted fish at all! The hot briquets coax out an enchanting aroma and turn the lustrous surfaces of the raw fish to a sizzling golden brown!

Gourmets insist that heads be left on. Tender-hearted diners prefer not to look the fish in the eye. The choice is yours to make.

When the briquets are coated with gray ash, knock off the ash and heap them slightly behind the spit. Place an aluminum foil drip pan (see page 15) in front of briquets. Rub the spit basket with cooking oil and put the spit basket on the spit rod. Arrange the fish in a single layer in the basket, alternating head and tail ends for better use of space. Use spit forks at the ends of the basket to hold the fish in place. Adjust the cover of the basket, being sure that it is not too tight, or it will tear the skin. Attach the spit and start the motor. Barbecue 10 to 15 minutes, depending on thickness of fish. Fish is done when it flakes easily with a fork. Baste, during the last 5 minutes, with melted butter or margarine. Before serving, sprinkle with salt and coarse, freshly ground black pepper.

Knock the fine gray ash off the charcoal briquets before starting to barbecue.

Tighten spit forks with pliers — otherwise they will be loosened by the heat.

Barbecued Large Whole Fish

A leviathan of a striped bass occupies the entire length of the spit as it rotates over charcoal to the flavor peak of doneness.

When you catch the one that usually gets away and triumphantly bring your record-breaker over the side of the boat, what a joy it is to remember that the Big Boy unit is ready to barbecue the fish on the revolving spit over hot charcoal briquets, to tender, flaky perfection! For a real treat, try it smoked.

Sea bass, tuna, bluefish, salmon, large mackerel, mullet, pike and weakfish are some of the fish you can barbecue, whole, on a spit. Clean a fish weighing 3 lbs. or more and remove the head. Using small, nail-size skewers and twine, lace up the cavity tightly. If the fish is a whopper, it may be advisable to tie it around the body with twine spaced at half-inch intervals for the entire length of the fish to prevent it from falling from the spit or breaking apart.

Place the fish on the spit and test for balance (see page 18). Be sure the tines of the spit forks are firmly inserted in the fish. Then heap the briquets slightly behind the spit and knock off gray ash. Place an aluminum foil drip pan (see page 15) in front of the briquets. Attach the spit and start the motor. During barbecuing brush the fish frequently with melted butter or margarine to keep the surface moist. The butter may be herb-flavored, if you like with marjoram, oregano or rosemary. Cook 20 to 40 minutes, depending on the size of the fish. Fish is done when it flakes easily with a fork. Remove from spit and sprinkle with salt and fresh, coarsely ground black pepper.

Big Boy Unit DL500

Barbecued Shish Kebob

*Romance of the Near East in your own back yard! Call them
shish kebob, kebabs, kabobs—what you please—the aroma of well-
marinated chunks of tender meat, skewered with bacon and vegetables, turning over hot briquets will bring guests running.*

Bacon-Wrapped Beef

Tomato

Green Pepper

Mushroom

Sweet Red Pepper

Bacon-Wrapped Beef

There is almost no limit to the variety you can
achieve in making shish kebob. The chosen foods
can be alternated on one skewer, as shown here,
or each type can be strung on a separate skewer.

Beef can be used instead of lamb, strung on the
skewer with bacon wrapped around it, and thick
slices of celery for a crisp, savory variation.

When barbecuing meats and vegetables together, you might use small pieces of meat and
large pieces of vegetables.

Vegetables alone can be skewered — mushrooms, small whole tomatoes, slices of green peppers and sweet red peppers, quartered
onions, sliced zucchini or summer squash .

Marinate the chunks of meat for several hours or longer in a well-
seasoned sauce such as Marinade on page 22. Brush kebobs with Marinade during the last 5 minutes of barbecuing. When barbecuing
vegetables alone, brush with Marinade after they are on the skewers.

A very hot fire is best for Shish Kebob. Place skewers 3 to 4 inches
above the briquets for best results. When using hand skewers, like the
one shown at the left, it is necessary to keep rotating them.

Teen-Age Party

A barbecue outfit at home will keep the kids "in their own backyard," busily cooking their favorite foods either for a family meal, or for a party of their own.

Hamburgers and hot dogs are favorite fare. If frankfurters are scored as shown above, they won't curl during barbecuing. Two or three to a "customer" is the rule. Four pounds of ground beef will make 20 large hamburgers.

Hamburger patties should be thick and they should be turned only once during barbecuing. If both hamburgers and frankfurters are barbecued at the same time, start the hamburgers first, as frankfurters are pre-cooked and need only to be heated and browned. Barbecuing time may vary (see page 13). Generally speaking, thick hamburgers require barbecuing about 10 minutes on one side and about 7 minutes after turning, to suit the average taste. When using a brazier, you can take some of the hamburgers off the grill when rare and continue to barbecue the rest to the medium or well-done stage as desired.

The Slant-Grill, Flip Grill and Flipper-ette are all perfect for barbecuing your hamburgers as well as frankfurters to a turn. However, each has its own special feature. With the Slant-Grill and Flip Grill, you can have rare, medium and well-done hamburgers ready to come from the grill at one time. With the Flip Grill and Flipper-ette, one flip of the grill turns all the meat. There's no more need to leave room for turning each piece.

Be sure to provide all the additional foods and relishes that make the kids happy. Sliced cheese for cheeseburgers, frankfurter and hamburger rolls, sliced onions and tomatoes, crisp lettuce, pickles, pickle relish, mustard, ketchup and other relishes. Mugs of milk are welcome. For dessert: cake, pie, cookies and ice cream or a luscious fruit shortcake will please everybody (see pages 60, 61).

Heavenly Hamburgers

Set out all the "makings" and "trimmings" so that the kids can feast their eyes while they compose their own barbecue masterpieces.

While hamburgers are very good indeed just cooked plain, the more adventuresome may want to try some innovations, such as the suggestions that follow:

Cheeseburgers: Barbecue hamburger on one side on the Flip Grill; turn; raise the top of the grill and place a slice of processed American cheese on top of each hamburger. When the under side is done, flip again and barbecue for a minute or so until the cheese begins to brown. Serve in toasted hamburger buns.

Hamburger Double Deckers: Make thin hamburger patties, about 1/4 inch thick. Put 2 together with any of the following fillings between. Barbecue on the Flip Grill about 14 to 16 minutes, turning once. Serve in hamburger buns.
1. A slice of processed American cheese spread with mustard and ketchup.
2. A thin slice of Spanish or Bermuda onion spread with chili sauce and sprinkled with sweet pickle relish.
3. A thin slice of tomato spread with mayonnaise and sprinkled with cut chives or minced onion.

Blunderburgers: These are featured by a New York hamburger restaurant, which informs the customer that the blunder occurred when the meat was left out!

Toast split hamburger rolls on cut side; spread with mayonnaise. Put together with a slice of cheese, a slice of tomato and half slices of crisp bacon. Barbecue on the Flip Grill until cheese melts.

Frankfurter Treats

A long-handled toasting fork with 4 tines makes it possible for several kids to "get in on the act," barbecuing hot dogs and toasting marshmallows to a delicate golden brown. Note spacing of briquets.

Hot dogs are every bit as versatile as hamburgers, so let the kids try some of these specialties:

Dixie Dogs: Split frankfurters lengthwise; spread cut surfaces with peanut butter; wrap in a strip of bacon. Barbecue on the Flip Grill until bacon is done as desired, turning once. Slide into toasted frankfurter roll.

Wisconsin's Pride: Split frankfurters lengthwise; insert a thin strip of processed American cheese, wrap in a strip of bacon. Barbecue on the Flip Grill until bacon is done as desired, turning once. Slide into toasted frankfurter roll.

Boston's Best: Split frankfurters lengthwise; spread cut surface with mustard; sprinkle with sweet pickle relish; fill with drained baked beans. Wrap each one securely in a double thickness of heavy duty aluminum foil, twisting the ends. Place on briquets and barbecue about 4 to 5 minutes, turning once. Unwrap and serve in toasted frankfurter rolls.

Coney Island Special: Split frankfurters lengthwise; spread with mustard; then with ketchup. Fill with drained sauerkraut. Wrap in a double thickness of heavy duty aluminum foil. Place on briquets and barbecue 4 to 5 minutes, turning once. Unwrap and serve in a frankfurter roll.

South-Of-The-Border: Barbecue frankfurters on the Flip Grill. Toast split frankfurter rolls on both sides. Arrange 2 halves of toasted rolls on each plate; top with hot chili con carne and 2 sizzling hot frankfurters.

Barbecued Corn

Select **tender sweet corn** in the husks. Strip husks down to end of cob. Do not tear off. Remove silk. If desired, let stand in **salted ice water** 20 minutes to 1 hour; then drain well. Brush corn with **softened butter or margarine** and sprinkle with **salt** and **coarse, freshly ground black pepper.** Bring husks up around corn. Be sure entire ear is covered. Kernels are exposed in pictures at left to illustrate the following barbecue methods.

METHOD 1. Prepare corn as above. Secure husks in 3 places with thin florist's wire. Lay corn on top of hot briquets and barbecue 10 to 12 minutes; turn a quarter turn 4 times during barbecuing. When corn is done, remove wire and husks. Serve at once.

METHOD 2. Prepare corn as above. Wrap each ear securely in a double thickness of heavy duty aluminum foil; twist ends well. Knock gray ash off the briquets. Lay corn on briquets. Barbecue about 10 minutes, turning once.

METHOD 3. Prepare corn as above. Slip spit rod through spit basket. Arrange the corn in basket. Put basket cover in place. Knock gray ash off briquets. Attach the spit and start the motor. Barbecue about 20 minutes.

Barbecued Potatoes

Piping hot, fluffy Barbecued Potatoes, topped with plenty of butter and served with charcoal flavored Barbecued Steak is a combination fit for a king.

Select **medium-size baking potatoes;** scrub well and pat dry with paper toweling. Rub the skins with **soft butter or margarine.** Wrap each potato tightly in a double thickness of heavy duty aluminum foil. Knock the gray ash off the briquets and lay potatoes on top. Barbecue medium-size potatoes 45 to 60 minutes; large potatoes 1 to 1¼ hours. Turn several times during barbecuing. Potatoes are done if they feel soft when gently pressed with an asbestos-gloved thumb. When soft, slit the foil, cut potato in both directions and press gently to break open. Fluff potato with a fork and season to taste with **butter or margarine, salt** and **coarse, freshly ground black pepper.** Or, top with a spoonful of **sour cream,** mixed with **finely chopped chives** or **grated onion.**

Barbecued Zucchini Creole

Slice **zucchini squash,** crosswise, in 1/4-inch slices. Place individual portions on double thicknesses of heavy duty aluminum foil. Add **cubed fresh tomato, sliced celery, salt, coarse, freshly ground black pepper,** a **dash of sugar** and a **pat of butter or margarine.** Wrap foil securely around food. Barbecue on briquets 14 to 16 minutes or on grill about 20 to 24 minutes, turning once.

Grilled Mushrooms

For each person, place about **6 medium-size mushrooms** in a square of doubled heavy duty aluminum foil. Add about **1½ tablespoons butter or margarine, few grains of salt and coarse, freshly ground black pepper.** Wrap foil around mushrooms. Barbecue on the grill about 4 minutes; turn and cook 4 minutes longer.

Stuffed Green Peppers

Cut a slice from the stem end of **8 green peppers;** remove white ribs and seeds. Place each on a double thickness of heavy duty aluminum foil. Fill with **canned chili beans.** Top each with **1 tablespoon ketchup.** Wrap securely in foil. Barbecue on briquets about 15 minutes or on grill about 30 minutes. Turn once during barbecuing.

Vegetable Medley

For each individual serving, make a 9″ square of a double thickness of heavy duty aluminum foil. On each square put **a slice of peeled, fresh tomato,** some **cubed, peeled, eggplant, a thin slice of Bermuda or Spanish onion, a sliced mushroom, a few frozen peas** and **pat of butter or margarine.** Sprinkle with **salt** and **fresh, coarsely ground black pepper.** Wrap tightly in the foil and barbecue on the briquets about 15 minutes, or on the grill 30 to 35 minutes. Turn once during cooking.

French Fried Potatoes

Use a 9-inch metal pie pan. (Or, for individual servings, use small aluminum foil pie pans.) Put **frozen French fried potatoes** in the pan and sprinkle with **salt.** Place pan on the grill very close to the briquets or directly on the briquets and barbecue 10 to 15 minutes or until hot and brown. Stir once while heating.

Barbecued Party Apples

Core **large baking apples.** Pare a third of the way down from stem end. Place each on a double thickness of heavy duty aluminum foil. Fill centers with a mixture of **sugar** and **cinnamon.** Brush peeled surfaces with **pink-tinted light corn syrup** and put about 1/2 **tablespoon butter or margarine** on each. Wrap very securely in foil. Barbecue 1 hour on grill or 25 to 30 minutes on briquets. Apples are done if they feel soft when gently pressed with an asbestos-gloved thumb.

Honey Grilled Pineapple

Cut **a medium-size fresh pineapple** into 8 lengthwise wedges. Place each wedge on a double thickness of heavy duty aluminum foil. Pour **1 tablespoon honey** over each. Allow to stand 1/2 hour. Wrap securely in the foil. Barbecue on grill 18 to 22 minutes or on briquets 14 to 16 minutes.

Hawaiian Oranges

For each serving, peel a **seedless orange** and separate into sections. Put each sectioned orange on a double thickness of heavy duty aluminum foil. Sprinkle generously with **brown sugar.** Add a **dash of cinnamon,** a **tablespoon of light rum** and a **teaspoon of butter or margarine.** Wrap securely in foil. Barbecue on the grill 12 to 15 minutes or on briquets 8 to 12 minutes.

Barbecued Spiced Bananas

Peel **bananas.** Place each on a double thickness of heavy duty aluminum foil. Brush with **lemon juice.** Sprinkle generously with **brown sugar;** dust with **cinnamon** or **nutmeg;** dot with **butter or margarine.** Wrap the foil securely around the bananas, twisting ends. Barbecue on grill 7 to 9 minutes or on briquets 4 to 5 minutes.

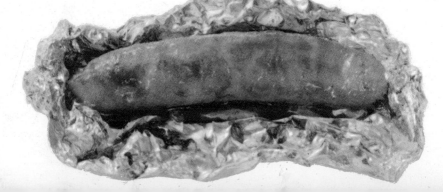

Cheese Topped French Bread

Cut a **loaf of French bread** in half, lengthwise. Brush generously with **melted butter or Garlic Butter** (recipe below). Sprinkle liberally with **grated Parmesan or sharp Cheddar cheese.** Put halves together; wrap securely in a double thickness of heavy duty aluminum foil. Place in the warming oven 15 to 20 minutes, on grill 10 to 12 minutes, or, on briquets, 6 to 9 minutes. To serve, slice crosswise, to make sandwiches.

GARLIC BUTTER: Place **1/4 pound butter or margarine** and **1 clove crushed garlic** in small saucepan at the edge of the grill where heat is low. When butter is melted, stir and cook 2 minutes. Do not let butter brown.

Fan Tan Garlic Rolls

Use **ready-to-serve or brown-and-serve packaged Fan Tan Rolls.** Remove rolls from the package and place on a double thickness of heavy duty aluminum foil. Brush liberally between cut sections and on top with **Garlic Butter** (recipe above). Wrap securely in foil. Place ready-to-serve rolls in the warming oven 15 to 20 minutes, on grill 10 to 12 minutes or on briquets 6 to 9 minutes. Place brown-and-serve rolls on the grill 20 to 25 minutes or on briquets 10 to 12 minutes.

Poppy Seed Bread

Use **a small loaf of unsliced white bread.** Cut in half lengthwise, almost through to bottom, then crosswise, in eighths. Place on a double thickness of heavy duty aluminum foil. Brush all cut and outside surfaces with **melted butter or Garlic Butter** (recipe above). Sprinkle top sides and cut surfaces liberally with **poppy seeds.** Wrap securely in foil. Place in warming oven 15 to 20 minutes, on the grill 10 to 12 minutes or on briquets 6 to 9 minutes. To serve, pull sections apart.

57

Fruit Spear Platter

A beautifully arranged platter of fresh fruit spears is simple to prepare and adds interesting color and texture to a meal. Try serving a platter of fruit in place of vegetables. The fruit is eaten as a finger food.

On a bed of **crisp salad greens** arrange **finger-size pieces of chilled watermelon, pineapple, cantaloupe or honeydew melon** and **bananas, thin unpeeled slices of red apples** and **quartered, cored, unpeeled pears;** place a small **whole pineapple** in the center of the platter, if desired. Provide small bowls of **French dressing, sour cream and cream mayonnaise** for "dunking," if desired.

Salad Dressing For Mixed Greens

1/2 pound Roquefort or blue cheese	3 tablespoons red table wine
1/4 cup lemon juice	2 teaspoons dry mustard
1/3 tube anchovy paste	2 teaspoons prepared mustard
1/4 cup tarragon vinegar	Salt to taste
2 tablespoons bottled thick steak sauce	Freshly ground black pepper
	2/3 cup olive oil
	2/3 cup salad oil
2 tablespoons Worcestershire sauce	2 garlic cloves, if desired

Put half the cheese in the large bowl of an electric mixer; beat until creamy. Blend in next 8 ingredients and salt and pepper to taste. Gradually add oils. Crumble an equal amount of remaining cheese into each of 2 pint jars with tight-fitting covers. Fill jars with dressing. Store in refrigerator. About an hour before serving, add a garlic clove to each jar and let stand at room temperature. To serve, shake thoroughly; pour over greens and toss. If desired, sprinkle with grated Parmesan cheese and add more salt and pepper. Makes about 2 pints.

Caesar Salad

Juice of 2 lemons
1/2 cup olive oil
1/4 cup wine vinegar
1 tablespoon Worcestershire sauce
2 whole garlic cloves, peeled
2 cups 1/2-inch bread cubes
2 garlic cloves, peeled and crushed
1/2 cup butter
4 heads crisp romaine*
2 eggs, raw or coddled 2 minutes
1/4 cup grated Parmesan cheese
1 small can anchovy fillets,
  whole or diced
Salt
Coarse, freshly ground black pepper

Combine first 5 ingredients; let stand several hours. Remove garlic.

Toast bread cubes on a baking sheet in a moderate oven, 350°F, stirring occasionally, until cubes are lightly browned on all sides. Melt butter with crushed garlic in a large frying pan, stir in toasted bread cubes; continue stirring until cubes absorb butter. Keep warm. Break romaine into a large salad bowl. Break eggs over the romaine; add olive oil mixture. Toss well until all traces of egg disappear. Add cheese, anchovy fillets, toasted cubes and salt to taste. Pepper generously with coarse, freshly ground black pepper. Toss again to mix. Makes 12 servings.

*Or 3 quarts shredded lettuce or mixed salad greens.

Golden Potato Salad

4 cups diced, cold boiled
  potatoes
1 small onion, chopped
2 tablespoons chopped parsley
1 cup chopped celery
1 teaspoon salt
2 tablespoons light cream

4 tablespoons yellow prepared
  mustard
2 tablespoons sugar
2 tablespoons vinegar
1/4 teaspoon salt
Dash pepper
Crisp salad greens

In a large bowl, put potatoes, onion, parsley, celery and the 1 teaspoon salt and toss lightly. Combine cream and next 5 ingredients and beat with a rotary beater until light and fluffy. Pour over the potato mixture and stir gently until well mixed. Let stand about 1 hour. Line a salad bowl with salad greens and arrange potato salad on top. Makes 6 to 8 servings.

Banana Walnut Chiffon Cake

2¼ cups sifted cake flour
1½ cups sugar
3 teaspoons baking powder
1 teaspoon salt
1/2 cup cooking oil
5 egg yolks, unbeaten
1 cup mashed ripe bananas
1 tablespoon lemon juice
1/2 teaspoon cream of tartar
1 cup egg whites
Whipped cream
Chopped walnuts

Set oven for moderately low, 325°F. Sift together flour, sugar, baking powder, and salt. Make a "well" in dry ingredients and add next 4 ingredients in the order listed. Beat until smooth. Add cream of tartar to egg whites and whip in a large mixing bowl until they form very stiff peaks. Gradually and gently fold flour mixture into egg whites, just until blended. Do not stir. Turn into an ungreased, 10-inch tube pan. Bake 1 hour and 5 minutes, or until top springs back when lightly touched with the fingertip. Invert pan; let cake hang until cold.

To remove, loosen from sides and tube of pan with spatula. Frost with whipped cream and garnish with nuts.

Chocolate Cake

2 cups sifted cake flour
2 teaspoons baking powder
1/2 teaspoon baking soda
1/2 teaspoon salt
1/2 cup shortening
2 cups firmly packed brown sugar

2 eggs
1 teaspoon vanilla
4 squares unsweetened
    chocolate, melted
1 cup plus 2 tablespoons milk
Coffee Frosting

Set oven for moderate, 350°F. Grease and flour two 8-inch round cake pans. Sift together flour, baking powder, baking soda and salt. Beat shortening; add sugar gradually; beat until fluffy. Add eggs, one at a time; beat well after each addition; stir in vanilla and chocolate. Add dry ingredients alternately with milk; stir only enough to blend well. Turn into pans. Bake 30 minutes or until cake springs back when lightly pressed with fingertip. Cool in pans 10 to 15 minutes. Remove; cool on a rack. Frost with Coffee Frosting.

COFFEE FROSTING: Combine 2 egg whites, 1½ cups sugar, 1/2 teaspoon cream of tartar, 1/3 cup strong coffee and 2 teaspoons light corn syrup in top of a double boiler, stir to blend well. Place over boiling water and beat with a rotary beater until frosting holds its shape. Remove from heat; continue beating until frosting stands in peaks.

Old-Fashioned Strawberry Shortcake

2 cups sifted flour
3 teaspoons baking powder
1/2 teaspoon salt
2 tablespoons sugar
1/2 cup shortening
1 egg, well beaten
1/3 cup milk (about)
2 quarts strawberries
Sugar
2 tablespoons butter or margarine
Sweetened whipped cream

Set oven for very hot, 450°F. Grease an 8-inch round cake pan.

Mix and sift flour, baking powder, salt and the 2 tablespoons sugar. Cut in shortening with a pastry blender or 2 knives until mixture looks like coarse cornmeal. Combine egg and milk; stir into flour mixture to make a soft dough. If dough is too stiff, add a little more milk. Pat or roll out into an 8-inch circle; place in pan. Bake 15 to 18 minutes, until brown.

Meanwhile, wash and hull berries; slice and sprinkle with sugar to taste.

When cake is done, remove from pan; split and spread with butter. Put lower half on a serving plate and cover with half the berries. Top with remaining cake and berries. Serve with whipped cream. Makes 6 to 8 servings.

Note: You may use two 10-ounce packages sliced frozen strawberries in place of the fresh strawberries.

Apple Pie

Pastry for a 2-crust pie or 1
   package pie crust mix
5 or 6 tart apples, pared and sliced
1 cup sugar

2 teaspoons flour
Dash nutmeg
1/2 teaspoon cinnamon
2 tablespoons butter or margarine

Set the oven for hot, 400°F.

Prepare pastry. Roll out half of it in a circle about 12 inches in diameter and 1/8 inch thick. Line a 9-inch pie pan with the pastry and trim 1/4 inch from rim. Arrange apples in pan. Mix sugar, flour and spices; sprinkle over apples. Dot with butter. Roll out remaining pastry about 11 inches in diameter and 1/8 inch thick. Cut slit for steam to escape. Adjust pastry over apples and trim 1/2 inch from rim of pan. Fold edge of top pastry under edge of lower pastry. Press edges together and flute or crimp. Bake 45 minutes or until crust browns and apples are tender.

Decorate the pie with "apples" cut from slices of processed cheese and sprinkled with paprika.

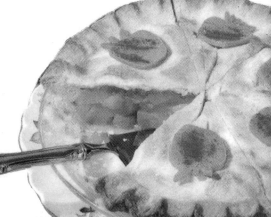

Care and Cleaning of Barbecue Equipment

The service you get from your barbecue equipment depends on the kind of care you give it. A few minutes time spent at regular intervals is all that is needed.

The secret to cleaning is promptness after each use. You'll be surprised how easy it is and how little time it takes.

Care of Equipment

On wagon-type units, occasionally oil axles of the wheels inside and outside and oil mechanism for adjusting position of fire box. On Slant-Grill, also, oil mechanism for adjusting grill position.

On braziers, occasionally oil the axles of the wheels inside and out. Apply oil frequently to the threads on the mechanism for raising and lowering the grill.

Before each use, remove dust from the equipment with a soft cloth.

At barbecuing time, before putting any food on the grill or in the spit basket, rub it with cooking oil or a piece of fat cut from the meat. This provides a protective coating and makes it easier to clean off burned juices and fats when barbecuing is done.

Cleaning of Equipment

THE EASY WAY: As soon as barbecuing is completed, lift the grill from the unit with an asbestos-gloved hand and rub the rods, top and bottom, with a large cloth dampened with cold water. This is especially important on the Slant-Grill, Flipper-ette and Flip Grill. If particles of burned juices and fats remain on rods, fat will drip on briquets instead of running off ends of rods. Also, wipe all other metal surfaces in the cooking area with a damp cloth. This takes only a few minutes.

Wash the spit basket, spit rods, spit forks and skewers in a pan of hot soapy water the same as you wash china or silver.

Occasionally clean the gravel as directed on page 9, paragraph 3.

THE HARD WAY: When the barbecue unit and grill have been permitted to cool, put the grill in a service sink. Scrub with a heavy duty brush and hot soapy water. With a cloth wipe all other metal surfaces in the cooking area.

Storage of Equipment

When cleaning is done, store Big Boy Equipment in a clean dry place. Use the special canvas cover to keep it dry and free from dust.

Proper care and cleaning of your barbecue equipment assures you the greatest amount of enjoyment and years of trouble-free barbecuing pleasure.

Index

Index

You Will Need An Aluminum Foil Drip Pan for these Recipes